What We Wear

Fiona Macdonald

FRANKLIN WATTS
NEW YORK • LONDON • SYDNEY

First published in 1998 by
Franklin Watts
96 Leonard Street
London EC2A 4XD

This edition published 2000
© Franklin Watts 1998

Franklin Watts Australia
14 Mars Road
Lane Cove
NSW 2006 Australia

Editor: Helen Lanz
Art Director: Robert Walster
Designer: Andy Stagg
Consultant: Cally Blackman,
MA History of Dress,
Courtauld

ISBN 0 7496 3150 3 (hbk)
      0 7496 2779 X (pbk)

Dewey Decimal
Classification Number: 391

Printed in Malaysia

Picture Credits
Cover images: Science and
Society Picture Library
(main image), Victoria
and Albert Museum (bl),
Image Bank (br).
Interior: Bubbles Photo
Library p. 6; Eye Ubiquitous
p. 14; Mary Evans Picture
Library p. 12l; Getty Images
pp. 4, 9r, 10l, 13, 15tl, 15br,
16r, 17, 21bl, 23t, 24, 25, 26,
28br; Robert Harding
Picture Library pp. 8br, 9tl;
Magnum Photos p. 21t;
National Trust Photographic
Library p. 11; Photofusion
p. 23bl, 29tr; Popperfoto
pp. 7, 20, 22, 28tl, 29cr;
Science and Society Picture
Library pp. 18, 19t; Topham
Picturepoint pp. 8tl, 27bl,
27tr; V & A Picture Library
pp. 3, 10br, 12r, 16bl; Franklin
Watts p. 19bl.

CONTENTS

Introduction

Today, many people like to wear **casual** clothes, such as T-shirts and jeans. Casual clothes are comfortable and easy to wear.

Casual clothes like these are *fashionable* today.

In the past, people's clothes were not as easy to wear. They were often thick and heavy, with stiff collars and tight-fitting waists.

TIME LINE

1900s   1910s   1920s   1930s   1940s

This family, photographed around 1900, are dressed in their *Sunday best*. It was thought to be fashionable then to wear stiff, *starchy* clothes.

This book will tell you what clothes were like long ago.

Look at this time line. It will tell you when the photographs showing the past were taken.

1950s   1960s   1970s   1980s   1990s   2000s

Clothes for a purpose

People wear clothes to suit what they are doing. They may wear special clothes, or **uniforms**, for work or school.

A uniform tells others a lot about the person who is wearing it. It may show what that person's job is, or if he or she belongs to a special club.

Some uniforms, such as these police uniforms from around 1900, have not changed much over the years.

These 1990s firemen are wearing special clothes to protect them from the heat of a fire.

(Above) Some children still wear school uniform today. How many differences can you see between the modern uniforms above and the one on the right?

This boy's school uniform, from around 1900, had knee-length trousers and a matching jacket and cap.

High society

People usually like to wear their best clothes for special occasions. It was the same in the past.

These people, photographed in 1912, are wearing the latest *fashions*.

Women often carried parasols (like umbrellas) to shade their faces from the sun.

People from high society (the rich and powerful) liked to dress smartly. Women wore long silk dresses. Men wore suits and tall black top hats.

Rich families also liked their servants to be smartly dressed. Most families do not have servants today.

Servants in a big house, around 1910. Many women servants had to wear aprons and caps. The men had to wear smart suits with starched collars.

Bright young things

From 1914 to 1918 there was a terrible war called the First World War. After the war was over, young people wanted to enjoy themselves.

They danced, played loud music, drove fast cars and wore exciting new styles of clothes. People called them 'bright young things'.

Elegant shoes like this were very popular in the 1920s.

In the 1920s, it was fashionable to wear real animal furs. Tight-fitting hats were also popular. They were called 'cloches', which is the French word for 'bell'.

These young men are wearing the latest
1920s fashions — hand-knitted jumpers,
short, baggy trousers called plus-fours,
and brightly-coloured woollen socks.

Sports clothes

Today, most people wear only a few, lightweight clothes when they play sport.

Modern sports clothes are made from stretchy **fabrics**, which make it easy for the person wearing them to move quickly.

Today, sports clothes use modern materials that are lightweight and allow the player to move easily.

In the past, sports clothes were much heavier, and more bulky. They did not stretch. It was difficult to move quickly in them.

TIME LINE

1900s   1910s   **1920s**   1930s   1940s

These tennis players were photographed around 1920. They are wearing jackets, scarves and knee-length skirts with thick stockings. Their sports shoes are quite small compared with the padded trainers people wear today, but they are still quite light.

These children are at the seaside, in 1927. Their knitted wool swimming costumes were heavy and baggy when they got wet. Can you imagine going swimming in these?

Thirties fashions

In the 1930s, fashions changed. Men and women no longer wanted to look like 'bright young things'. Instead, they wanted to look elegant.

Women wore tight dresses, and smart little hats. They liked smooth, short hairstyles, and carefully made-up faces.

This woman, photographed in 1934, is wearing a slim-looking suit with a neat, fitted jacket and high-heeled shoes.

Shoes like these were fashionable in the 1930s.

TIME LINE

| 1900s | 1910s | 1920s | **1930s** | 1940s |

Men wore close-fitting, or **tailored**, suits. Most suits had three matching parts: jacket, trousers and waistcoats. Many men chose to wear a hat when they were outside.

Young men wearing tailored suits in 1933. The man on the right is wearing a straw hat, called a boater, and the other men are wearing hats made from boiled, pressed wool, called felt.

Clothes in wartime

During the Second World War (which lasted from 1939 to 1945) cloth, buttons and thread were needed to make uniforms for soldiers. Clothes for women and children were in short supply.

In wartime, children wore home-made clothes sewn from left-over material.

To stop people wasting cloth, the government made laws that said clothes had to be plain and simple. Sayings such as 'make-do-and-mend' told people to look after the clothes they already had.

TIME LINE

1900s   1910s   1920s   1930s   **1940s**

(Above) The most fashionable clothes in the 1940s looked rather like uniforms.

(Left) To make sure there were enough clothes to go round, people were rationed, or limited, in the number of clothes they could buy. They were given a ration book.

1950s 1960s 1970s 1980s 1990s 2000s

Forties fashions

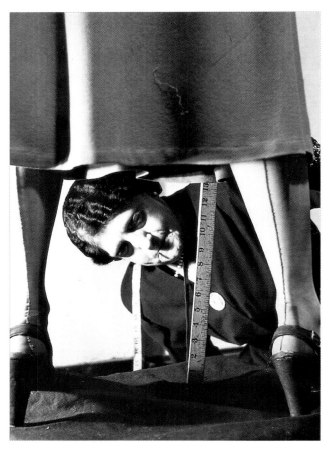

By the end of the Second World War in 1945, women were tired of wearing trousers and short, plain dresses. They were excited when a French fashion **designer**, called Christian Dior, created the 'New Look' in 1947.

A dressmaker checks that the *hem* is level on a New Look skirt in **1948**.

Dior's clothes had long, full, swirling skirts, tight-fitting tops, and tiny waists. Women loved wearing the New Look and other **glamorous** fashions of the late 1940s.

TIME LINE

1900s 1910s 1920s 1930s **1940s**

This woman, photographed in 1947, shows off a New Look dress.

Children's clothes in the 1940s were also much more glamorous. This girl's shorts and top have a matching skirt that can be kept on or taken off.

Rebel fashions

In the 1950s, teenage fashions were based on styles worn by two groups of young people called Teddy Boys and Beatniks.

Beatniks and Teddy Boys were **rebels**. They wanted to break the rules about what were the 'right' or 'wrong' things to wear. The clothes they wore showed which group they belonged to.

Today, young people still like to try out new styles of clothes.

Beatniks dressed in dark clothes. Girls often wore patterned short skirts. Heavy coats were also part of the look.

TIME LINE

| 1900s | 1910s | 1920s | 1930s | 1940s |

Teddy Boys photographed in 1955. Their long jackets had velvet collars and they wore tight trousers. Their hair was short and brushed back from their faces.

Rebels in the 1980s chose the *punk* style. Punks dyed their hair and wore a lot of leather with studs on.

1950s   1960s   1970s   1980s   1990s   2000s

Science and fashion

By the 1960s, many new types of cloth had been developed from **artificial** fibres. These materials were soon used in fashionable clothes.

Plastics were used to make shiny, waterproof coats and boots. They were also used to make exciting, bright-coloured jewellery.

In the late 1960s, plastic jewellery was popular. It was also fashionable to have short hair and to wear heavy black eye make-up.

TIME LINE

1900s	1910s	1920s	1930s	1940s

New stretchy, knitted fabrics were used to make close-fitting miniskirts and dresses. These came high above the knee.

Tights made from an artificial fibre called nylon were worn under miniskirts and dresses.

This young woman, photographed in **1967**, is wearing a knitted minidress and shiny plastic boots. She has *backcombed* (fluffed-up) hair which was a popular style in the 1960s.

Love and peace

This young woman is wearing a 'cat suit' (a close-fitting overall) with wide flared trousers. It is painted with a bright 'pop-art' pattern — and the car is painted to match.

In the 1960s, people wanted to live in a peaceful, loving world. They liked to do peaceful things like listening to music or trying out new ideas in art. They also wore a style of clothes to show their peaceful views.

Young women wore loose, flowing dresses or chose bright, **pop-art** styles.

TIME LINE

| 1900s | 1910s | 1920s | 1930s | 1940s |

(Right) Fashions of the 1970s.

(Below) Today, many people enjoy wearing styles from the 1960s and 1970s, such as minidresses and platform shoes.

In the 1970s, fashions changed. Both men and women wore flared trousers and platform shoes.

Many styles from the past have come back into fashion today.

Useful words

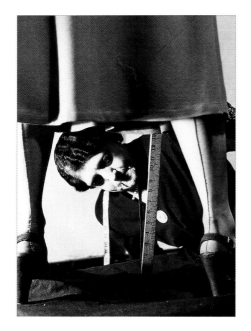

artificial: here, something that is not made from natural fibres.

backcombed: when hair is combed backwards (from the tip to the root) to make it fluff out.

casual: free and easy, rather than formal.

designer: someone who thinks of new ideas for clothes and draws them to show how they should be made.

fabrics: the different materials and cloth from which clothes are made.

fashion: clothes which are very popular at one particular time. Most fashionable clothes are usually popular for only a short while, before new styles come along.

fashionable: when something is in the most up-to-date style.

glamorous: smart and beautiful.

hem: the turn-up of material at the bottom of a skirt or dress.

pop-art: a fashion in the 1960s to paint images in an unexpected and modern way, often using bright colours.

punk: a rebel fashion of the1980s.

rebel: someone who goes against the rules.

Sunday best: clothes worn on Sundays and on special occasions.

starch: a vegetable powder that is mixed into a paste and used to stiffen clothes.

tailored: smart, close-fitting clothes, originally made by skilled craftworkers, called tailors, who made men's suits.

uniforms: special clothes that are worn to show that you go to a certain school or do a certain job.

Index